T0368463

AuthorHouse™
1663 Liberty Drive
Bloomington, IN 47403
www.authorhouse.com
Phone: 1 (800) 839-8640

Published by AuthorHouse 12/07/2015

ISBN: 978-1-5049-6565-1 (sc)
ISBN: 978-1-5049-6597-2 (e)

authorHOUSE®

Fun With Corks, After the Wine!

by   ***V. Darlene Geiser***

photos by Terry Geiser

About the author

Darlene Geiser, is a passionate horsewoman and animal enthusiast, born at Jacksonville Beach, Florida on Thanksgiving Day in the 50's. She dedicated her career as a Police Sergeant in Jacksonville, Florida to the people and animals she loves. After retiring, she continued teaching Mounted Police Operations as President of Geiser Equine, Inc., which was accredited by the University of Louisville's Southern Police Institute in Kentucky. This included writing instructional manuals for law enforcement. She also composed and illustrated a children's safety activity book featuring Mounted Police, as well as numerous published articles.

She was blessed with the talent of art and at an early age her father, being an artist himself, taught her to express her feelings on canvas.

At the age of eight she won her first art contest and excelled from that point and learned through art, she could support her horse habit and have all the animals she desired. Dreams do come true with hard work as she and her husband currently live on their central Florida horse farm with their animal family.

"I've always had a belief that if I see it, I too can do it!" She exclaimed, "I will try anything creative and add my own expression to it. I believe in everyone there is an artist anticipating unique expression of their own."

With this belief she tries to instill in others to find themselves. "Creating something that puts a smile on faces is most rewarding," She expresses from the heart.

"In today's stressful world, art is the best medicine. Relieve your stress, relax and create," She encourages

Photo by Bob Morgan

"I hope you enjoy creating art from wine corks and have as much fun as I have. And thank you for taking the time to share some fun, just you and me!" Enjoy,

V. Darlene Geiser

Dedication

To all who enjoy wine and the multitudes of wineries worldwide, especially those who are so proud of their product to create a printed cork. We applaud you!

These distinctive corks are what makes our art creations fun! Memories of good times are captured celebrating memorialized dates such as birthdays, anniversaries, promotions and any other momentous occasion.

Also to you, the crafter and artist who create beautiful pieces for all to enjoy! Let's have some fun together and make someone smile.

Various Animal Rescues and animals in need always receive a percentage of Darlene's art income.

Let's make them happy too! Furry smiles!

Acknowledgements

The greatest appreciation goes to my husband of 4 decades, Terry Geiser. He has supported all my efforts in numerous projects and continues to do so. He is truly a partner, from first being my Police patrol partner, to the love of my life. Without his support I wouldn't have accomplished the numerous goals set before me.

I also depend on a very special person, my sister Rita, who is my most important fan. I value so much her support and her keen eye as a critic to my work. She reviews the text for correctness with an objective eye. Without her I would not feel satisfied presenting this to you. She has always been a contributor to my cork collection, as a world traveler, and an educator in wine selections.

I want to express appreciation to our good friends, Ethna and Chris who own Lynches Pub & Grub in St. Armand's Circle at Sarasota, Florida. They have enjoyed my projects and supplied thousands of those used wine corks. To many more "Happy Hours", Thank you girlfriends!

All the art within these pages is in the memory of my beautiful artist niece, Rhonda, who forever inspired the creative gift in everyone she met.

1978 - 2013.

For More Information

Darlene always enjoys hearing from you, thus questions or expressions can be routed to Darlene at …

e-mail address: vdgauthorartist@aol.com and on Facebook

P.O. Box 960

Fairfield, Florida 32634-9700

Table of Contents

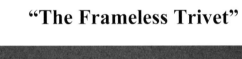

"The Frameless Trivet"

"The Serving Tray"

"The Wine Crate Shelf"

"Wall Art Hangings"

Basic Cork Boards to Décor Inserts!

"Textured Wall Art"

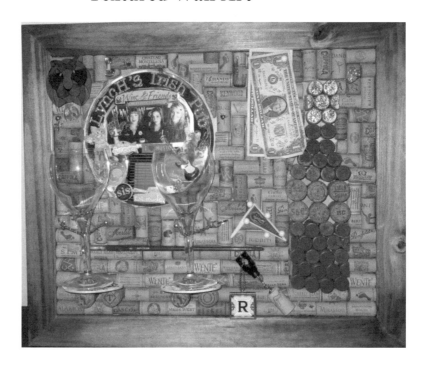

"The Message Board"

"The Circular Frame"

Mirrors, Photos and Clocks

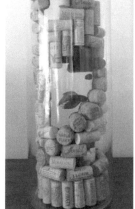

"Cork Castle Aquarium"

Introduction

<u>**Most Important…don't purchase screw top or box wines!**</u>

Between these pages you will discover easy, fun and useful craft projects for "Wine Cork Décor" which includes:

Trivet	Glass Cork Decor
Serving Tray	Wine Crate Shelf
Wall Art Hangings	Textured Wall Art
Mirror, Photo and Clock Frames	Message Board

Cork Castle Aquarium

Today's wine enthusiasts are everywhere and everyone loves to read the corks! Wine corks are fun and express the adventurous urge in most. Trying different wines to discover your own special taste can make a special celebration come to life. It's not unusual for that special cork to be saved as a memento to the occasion.

After you discover the fun of creating wine cork art, I think you will be looking at bottles of wine with a new eye. I find myself now reading labels and looking for the printed corks before purchasing, to tickle my taste buds.

Others also enjoy reading the corks, so glue the brand and/or logo to the outside and use as many different brands as possible. Be diversified. Your friends will love it!

Organized wine tasting is a popular social event today. There are many wine and cheese establishments in most communities which encourage a sip of various brands and vintages for your pallet. Usually these social events are held around the holiday season or a special occasion. Enjoy and collect the corks!

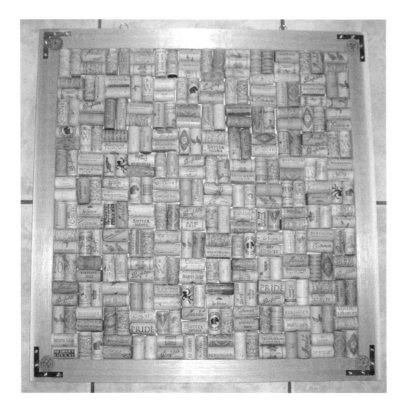

Decide on a project with these questions:

What is your skill level?

How many corks are needed and how do they fit together?

What item do you desire to make for your décor or a gift?

Skill Level

Be honest with yourself. Start simple. This instruction manual is designed so that Project One is the beginning of the skill levels. Start simple to attain the most enjoyment.

Have a cork party and enjoy crafting with friends!

Your Tool Box

Crafting tools and supplies needed:

Used wine corks, both natural and synthetic. Save them all!

Champagne corks   Needle-nose pliers'

Hot glue melting pot/hot glue gun   Small pliers'

Glue sticks   Small hammer

Wood glue   Tacks

Plastic gloves   Wall screws

Picture hanger kit   Cutting tool

Roll of paper towels   Cutting Board

Embellishments: Ceramic tiles or your choice of décor item inserts

Crafting Area Needs:

Have a table at least two feet by four feet, which allows plenty of layout room. A piece of cardboard or cover for the table would be best as the hot glue may drip onto the surface.

An electrical outlet nearby or an extension cord, is needed for the hot glue gun and melting pot.

Several trays for supplies and separation of the corks will make for easier selection and placement onto the project.

You may want a very comfortable chair, as well. I know once you get started, you will continue having so much fun that time will slip away.

Lighting is extremely important, thus have direct overhead lamps available.

Wine Corks

Wine corks are not all the same size. This is the reason for the separation trays in your work space. I've discovered four trays are needed; three for the wine corks and one for the Champagne corks. They should be separated in lengths, as such:

1. Large corks are 2" long
2. Average corks are 1 ¾" long
3. Short corks are 1 5/8" long
4. Champagne corks are round, but can be cut in all shapes

Note: If you are doing a project which only allows Natural corks, then pull the synthetic corks out and place them in another tray. You may desire an extra tray, as well for colored corks. Projects can be enhanced with the specific placement of the colored corks, such as choosing red and black corks together for perhaps a Georgia Bull Dogs fan or Orange and Blue for a Florida Gators fan. Colorful pieces are always exciting!

This one displays sea shells found by a beach bachelor who attended both the Universities. A verity of wines always makes for a more masterful art piece.

I've also discovered that with the larger projects, it is much easier to have the corks divided even in smaller groups than suggested, such as into natural and synthetic brands with the size differences. Below are 14 containers as an example. Just don't let the dog or cat flip the bowls!

This separation saves time once a project begins to take shape.

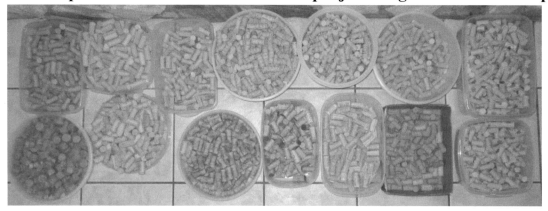

A. Number of Corks per project

The Number of Corks needed per project will depend on your chosen pattern. The following project sizes will assist you in order to determine that decision with your inventory of corks.

Size	Number of Corks Required
7" x 9"	45
8" x 8"	50
9" x 32"	185
10" x 13"	75
14" x 24"	168
20" x 20"	210
23" x 17"	270
24" x 24"	288
24" x 48"	650

<u>Note:</u> If your project has an insert, be sure to subtract the number of corks in that space. For example, a 6" x 6" tile would occupy spaces for 32 to 36 corks, depending on cork sizes.

B. Cork Design Patterns

There are eight basic patterns you can choose from for your design. With these you may enhance the pattern for your own personal touch. In some patterns there may be a space for embellishment or you may wish to leave spaces for your particular item. Be creative and unique!

These examples are not glued. They are simply set as you would do to decide which pattern best fits your project. When you have decided on a pattern there are some things to remember such as:

1. Place the corks with the brand names of the wines in a readable position.

2. Have different brands or logos next to each other.

3. Place natural and synthetic corks side by side instead of having all natural in one area and all synthetic in another.

You want the viewer's eye to flow over your entire work of art!

The number of corks needed for each pattern may also determine your choice depending on how many are available. In the pattern examples for this 7" x 9" inside frame measurement, I have given you the number of corks required. Remember, if you are lacking only a few corks, leave spaces and embellish!

For the rectangle or square there are six patterns. Circle patterns for a 12" diameter disc can use between 18 to 50 corks depending on your design and insert. It is primarily for clocks, photos and seasonal wreaths. The example for you is to create a fun clock using 30 wine corks, two champagne corks and a Tequila cork.

Rectangle or Square Project Patterns

1.   **Stack bond**

The Stack bond pattern above uses all full size corks. There are 45 within this frame.

2.   **Basket Weave**

The Basket Weave enhances the different brands of corks, however fitting may require different sizes and perhaps cutting of some. There are 40 full corks in this pattern.

3.   **Running bond**

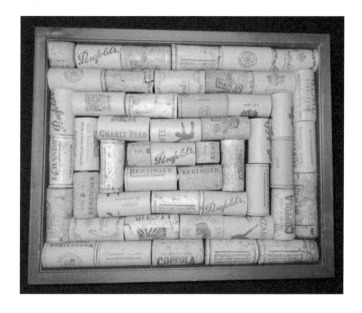

The Running bond takes some creative matching to complete each line and the corners. You will notice I had to cut some corks to fit, however, it does give a nice dimension to the piece. There are 47 corks of various sizes and 4 half corks, thus 49 corks are required.

4.   **Subway**

In the Subway you will notice the brick like pattern, however you can see on the right how the cut corks are used to finish the line. This would be done on the left side, as well. You will need 41 full corks and 8 half corks for a total of 45 corks.

5.   Herringbone

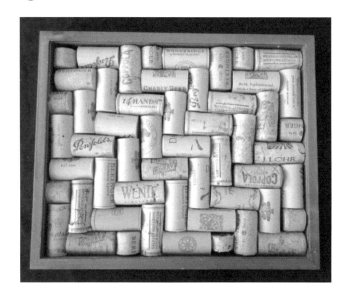

The Herringbone is one of my favorites. This pattern gives the viewer a flow from corner to corner of the frame. It's great for inserts or embellishments! You will need to cut corks for tight fits. There are 45 full corks of various sizes and 9 half corks, thus 49 ½ corks were used.

6.   Spiral

The Spiral pattern is very attractive, but can be difficult to attain the perfect fit, however the spaces between allow for some exciting embellishments. Fill them with glass tiles, champagne corks, etc… Here are 42 full corks and 3 half corks, thus 43 ½ corks are needed.

Let's review comparing the corks required for a design of the same dimensions, as in this 7" x 9" space and review the pattern choices:

Basket Weave	40 corks
Spiral	43 1/2
Subway	45
Stack Bond	45
Running Bond	49
Herringbone	49 ½

Circle Patterns for Photo Frames, Clocks or Wreaths

Now comes the more difficult but exciting circle patterns. These patterns can be used for seasonal decorations, as well as the examples shown. Circle patterns can be in door wreaths with some elaborate embellishments. Just let your imagination fly!

These displays, as well are not glued, but simply set for your viewing. They are on a 12" diameter circle wooden disc which can be purchased at any craft or hobby store.

7.   Circle Stack

The Circle Stack is great for picture frames, mirrors or clocks. Make sure the inside diameter is open enough for your insert, as you should glue the corks on the edge first. On this 12" diameter disc I have used 33 full corks on its rim.

8.   Circle Sunray

This pattern is again, great for inserts of photos, mirrors or clocks. You will have spaces shown so the base surface should be painted or stained. The smaller ends of the corks are to be placed to the inside of the circle in order to lessen the spaces on the outside of the circle of corks. For this 12" diameter disc I used 34 full corks.

C. Acquiring Your Wine Corks

There are many sources or means for acquiring wine corks, of which most are fun and interesting. If you are a do it yourself kind of person and only want to use corks you personally acquire, you may want to limit your projects to those needing fewer corks! It could take a long time to gather what you need, thus I suggest to combining the wine corks with other items in your craft project.

For larger projects, enlisting the help of family and friends is a good means to collect wine corks. This could seriously increase your cork stash in no time. After all, the efforts are for a good cause. Variety of cork brands is important in any project as you don't want the same brands or logos over and over and side by side. You will find that many people only drink one brand, thus make some new and more friends for diversity in wines. They must know your friendship depends on giving you all their used corks! Host a wine tasting and keep all the corks. "BYOW and leave the Cork" should be written on the invitation! ENJOY! This is a social event and only sips are allowed! It's a "Girlfriend Thing"!

Rita, Alison, Darlene and Felicia

Another very successful means of wine cork collecting is to visit some of your local wine serving and selling establishments to inquire about them saving you the corks. This will help you ensure a large amount and variety in the brands. You may have to promise some wine cork art for their wall, but don't worry. With this agreement you will have more than enough corks to make any project!

Finally, but not near as much fun, you can purchase used wine corks of varying sizes and brands at many of the commercial craft stores and the internet. There may be less than ten in a package. I have already shown you how many corks required to complete a small project. This method could be costly.

I personally prefer a combination of the first three methods of acquiring used wine corks. These are "Do it Yourself", wine tasting with Family and Friends and requests to Wine establishments.

Note: When making friends, ask if they drink wine and what brands do they like? Make sure it's a brand different from all the corks you already have. If not, influence them to go for the "Wild Side" and be adventurous in their wine tasting. I've noticed most Wineries are now being extremely creative with their labels and the names are rather interesting, as well. Go Shopping! Take a friend and have some fun!

Should you purchase a wine with an interesting label and discover no printing on the cork, don't despair. Blank corks are great for cutting to fill those small spaces in your craft. You will need them.

Be inspiring to your friends…

While collecting, however many corks your goal may be, display them in beautiful glass containers. Everyone will have fun adding more to your stash when entering your home. I have used attractive colored glass flower vases as they look beautiful with no expense. When someone wants to send you flowers, ask for colored glass!

Another idea in display is to take a round bowl aquarium, without the fish, place your arrangement of a candle, plant or other object in the center and surround the item with the wine corks. Be creative and embellish for each season.

This can be really simple and a beautiful accent to a table and your home. Light your candle or arrange your plant. Done! Enjoy and relax.

Should there be home front conversation about the means of wine cork collecting, be sure to also save, from the "Man-Cave" the various decorative wooden blend corks. They go nicely in a large glass beer mug! This may change the conversation your way.

No more arguments about your wine tasting experiences!

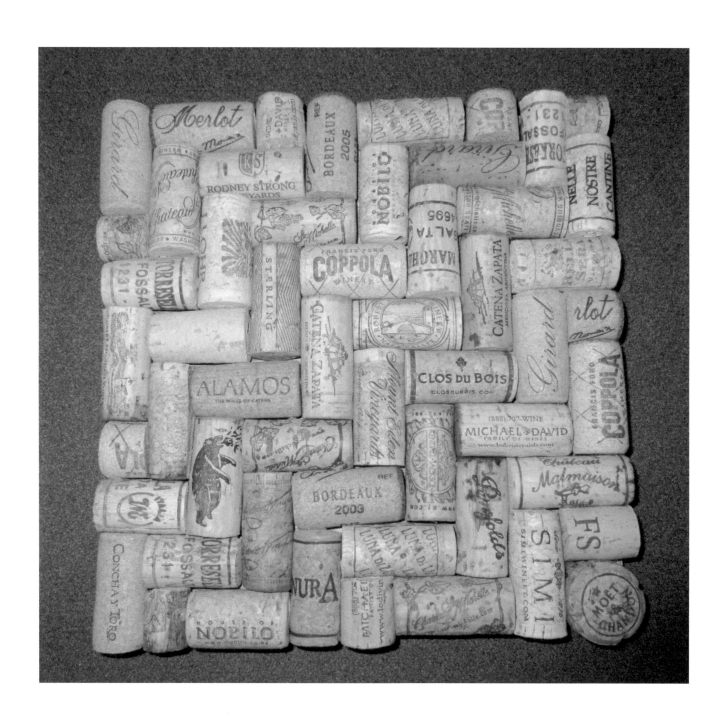

Project #1:   The Frameless Trivet

The average size of a trivet is an 8" x 8" square. It will be made with all natural corks, for your first easy project.

Needs: 8" x 8" thin board, Lauan plywood board is best. Lauan board can be cut with a razor knife for smaller pieces.. Be sure to sand the edges.

"50" Natural corks…..<u>NO synthetic corks</u> due to the hot dishes melting them. (Remember to always allow extra corks, thus have "55" available). You may also use champagne natural corks if you desire.

Hot glue melting pot

Glue sticks

Needle-nose pliers'

Cutting tool

Cutting board

Plastic gloves

Small wood pegs

Sand paper

Sticks approximately 10"long

Hanger, (optional)

Wooden Pegs

READY………………...SET……………………..GO!

1.   Pick your design and lay it out onto the wood. The corks should extend over the 8" x 8" board edge, as you do **not** want to see the backing board when this is completed.

Herringbone Pattern Layout

(Sticks are used to hold the corks for the layout. Optional)

2.   Put on your plastic gloves. Don't burn your fingers!

3.   Melt the glue sticks in the pot.

4.   Dip the cork's side into the glue pot with the needle-nose pliers'

and place the cork on the board. Corks will extend over the raw board edge.

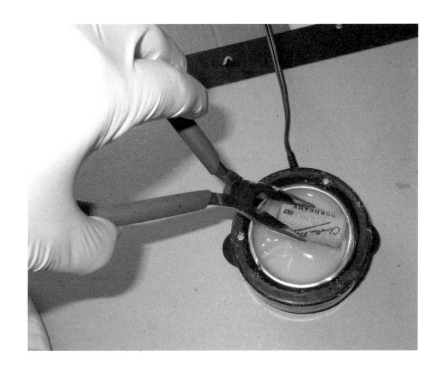

5. You may have to cut some corks in half to fill all spaces.

6. Turn the finished trivet over and hot glue the pegs at each corner. The pegs prevent the trivet from scratching the counter surface.

7. A nice touch is an attached hanger for the kitchen wall.

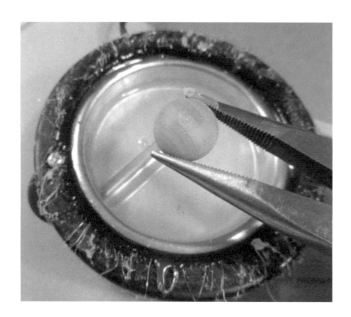

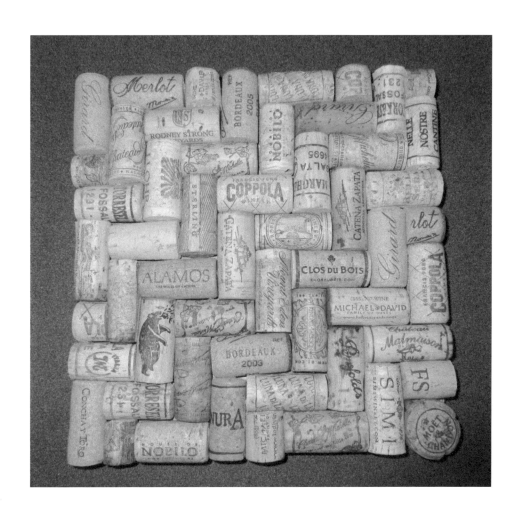

OKAY - YOU ARE DONE!   EASY…..QUICK……AND…….FUN!

CONGRATULATIONS ON YOUR FIRST PROJECT!

You have created a beautiful and useful item.

Lots of compliments coming your way.

Project #2:   The Serving Tray and the Wine Crate Shelf

The Serving Tray starts with the unfinished wooden tray purchased at your favorite craft store. These trays come in various sizes and shapes, ovals to rectangles.

In order to complete this project I'm using a rectangle tray, measuring 10" x 13"which will be hand painted with the grape leaf design as the oval tray above. This is where your artistic talent comes in to play!

The wine crate also is in a rectangle and sides are framed. Of course the dimensions vary with the brand of wine. These empty used crates can be purchased at wine retailers, or go for it and buy a new case! These are larger and require more corks, but the same basics are used for its creation.

Decide what color and theme this tray will be and its use. You may stain or paint the finish and paint or decoupage on the outside. I like to use the product, MOD PODGE® to decoupage. For this project I chose to dark stain the entire tray and paint grape vines on the outside. This one is to be for serving cheese and crackers to my guests with the various wines, as in hosting the wine tasting event.

The same staining and painted design can be done with the wine crate for your shelf. This shelf is for my husband's collection of shot glasses. The grooves in the wine crate accompany a glass shelf.

The above tray or wine crate finished with embellishments.

Let's get started on your Serving Tray!

Needs: For the 10" x 13" Tray, you will need…

<u>75 Corks</u>, *Remember, if it is for hot items, NO synthetic corks!*

Hot glue melting pot

Glue sticks

Needle-nose pliers'

Cutting tool and board

Plastic Gloves

Stain or paint with brushes

MOD PODGE® (optional)

Clear Satin Urethane Spray

Embellishments, (if desired)

1. The outside (Not the inside) of the tray will need to be sprayed with a sealer after you have stained and/or painted your design, if you desire. I like to use Clear Satin Urethane spray, which can be purchased at your favorite craft store. Prepare your frame first!

2. Arrange the corks in a pattern you choose. Try several, as all spaces must be filled and the frame is stationary, thus it may require cutting some corks. Be creative with your arrangement.

3. Dip the cork's side into the hot glue melting pot holding the cork with the pliers'. Place each into your pattern on the tray.

Note: In the framed serving tray, it would be better to have small spaces along the frame instead of between the corks. Items will be sitting on the corks and the less spaces, the more even the surface.

CONGRATULATIONS………..YOU DID IT!

You are now moving forward with your skill level to your artistic side.

The next project indulges your creative urges. Go for it!

Notes and Ideas:_____

_____

_____

_____

Indulge Yourself!

Project #3:   Wall Art Hanging

Art in reference to this manual, refers to creative ideas with a theme. Knowing who this art will be presented to and what subject that person loves most will guide your imagination. Fortunately wine brands comply with most topics of interest. It may be nature, nautical, equestrian, social or specific quality brands your recipient enjoys. Color may also be of interest, representing something really important in his or her life. This is depicted in the art piece for the beach bachelor's condo on page 17.

There are several Design Choices:

1.   Solid corks within a frame.
2.   Corks with painted tiles inserted, which can be a logo or design.
3.   Corks with a plaque item or floral such as grapes

The Size of your wall art will be determined by the:

1.   Amount of corks available
2.   Size of the crafter's desired décor insert

Needs:

Frame only, without glass

Lauan board to fit the back of the frame

Wood glue, tacks and a hammer to attach the backboard

Corks – natural and synthetic used wine corks

Tile, plaque or item desired for the insert design

Hot glue gun or Hot glue melting pot and glue sticks

Needle nose pliers'

Cutting board, to size the corks for a tight fit

Sand Paper

Straight Sticks

MOD PODGE®

Cutting tool

Picture hanger kit

Plastic Gloves

Spray sealing or paint

READY…………………..SET……………………..GO!

Prepare the Frame

Frames can be purchased at any craft or hobby retailer. They may be finished or not, depending on your project's requirement. No glass is needed and the frame will be without a backing. You must add the backing as this will be your gluing surface.

1. Cut the Lauan plywood Board to fit to the edges of the frame back.(1, 2, 3)

2. Sand the backing board edges. (4)

3. With the wood glue, glue the Lauan board to the frame.(5, 6)

4. After gluing the Lauan board, tack the board down. The tacks should not go through to the frame's front side. Wipe the excess glue from the edges as the stain or paint will not cover it.(7, 8, 9)

5. Now you are ready to stain or paint your frame if it is not already a finished surface. You may also want to seal it with a polyurethane spray or paint. Let dry.(10, 11, 12)

<u>Note:</u> Do not attach the picture hanger kit until the project is finished as the board must lay flat for it to be completed.

1.   2.   3.

4.   5.   6.

7.   8.   9.

10.   11.   12.

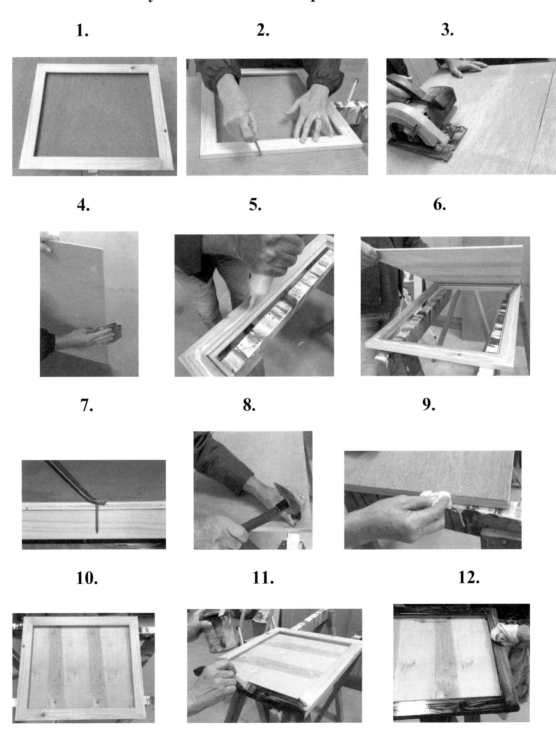

Prepare the insert

Paint or glue the art onto the tile or wood. Should you decide to insert a photo or print onto this surface, I suggest using MOD PODGE®. Cover the insert surface, then place the picture onto it and paint this goo over the entire surface. Don't worry, it dries clear!

Prepare the plaque, engraving, etc…

1. Attach the insert item or items before gluing the corks.

2. Glue the insert item or items onto the board. It would be best to use a wood or craft glue depending on the weight of the insert.

Deciding on a cork pattern

Note: After gluing the inserts onto the board, the design of the corks may change, so now try your patterns again, before gluing.

The above Basket Weave pattern is using 213 corks, for this 23" x 17" inside frame measurement with two inserts.

Refigured herringbone pattern above.

In this case, I decided on a Herringbone Pattern to express the "Fox Hunt" as I liked the flow of the hunt to the fox with the corks. This pattern will use 208 full corks with 10 ½ half corks or a total of 218 ½ corks. The Herringbone Pattern will require more corks than the other patterns.

1. Melt glue sticks in the pot. A hot glue melting pot is the easiest means of attaching the corks.

2. Using the needle-nose pliers', dip each cork on its side, into the hot glue and place it in the design selected. Start on the center of this space as you want as many full corks as possible for the pattern's effect. The half corks will fill in the spaces on the edges and be unnoticeable.

3. Continue filling the board with corks until all spaces are covered with whole corks. Cut whole corks to fill smaller spaces.

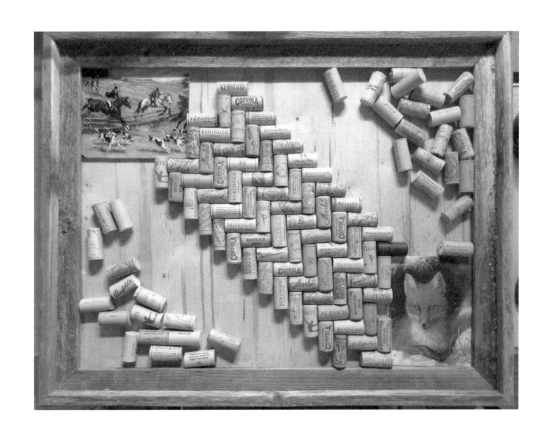

Again, you can see using straight sticks holds pattern lines.

Now your creative style comes into play. Everyone likes embellishments! Whatever your theme, your creative piece, can now expand to, WOW!

Note: Think of the items related to your inserts. These would be attachable items to draw attention to the theme.

_____

_____

_____

As you can see, the saddle leather and stirrup accent the horse bit. The "Hunt" print, saddle iron, bit and the fox print make a complete masterpiece. Our fox has escaped and living happily ever after!

Finally, attach the picture hanger kit, after determining the completed weight.

WOW! ………..YOUR   DONE – HANG   IT   UP!

You will soon be requested to do Special gifts for your friends. These Custom pieces are family treasures and loved by all.

Take it to an art show, as you created it!

Following are several examples of custom projects I've completed. Enjoy. You too, will want to create your own designs.

Usually these items have special meaning and the person requesting the art, provides corks from meaningful celebrations.

The Sheriff's Aviation Board, for a Deputy Pilot

It's best to start the Basket Weave pattern at the frame's edge and continue in straight lines, as you can see in this board.

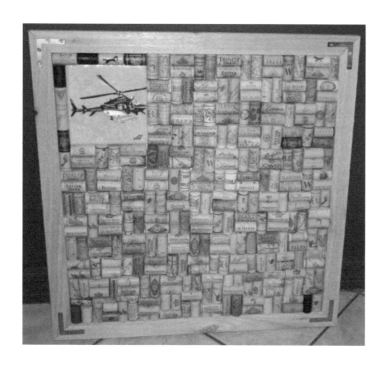

This Sheriff's Aviation Board of 21" x 22" inside measurement with a 6" x 6" hand painted tile insert, used 266 corks. Notice how the green colored corks are around the green and white helicopter tile to accent the colors and keep the eye flowing over the board.

I also placed the horse logo cork above this tile, as the Deputy pilot is a horseman. Know the recipient of your work. It does make a difference!

The following Dressage Horse Board of 18 ½" x 18 ½" inside with the 6" x 6" hand painted tile insert, used 185 full corks and 17 cut corks. Again notice the red cork placed by the insert to accent the red in the horse's head.

Colored corks are an exciting way to draw attention to your artist technique.

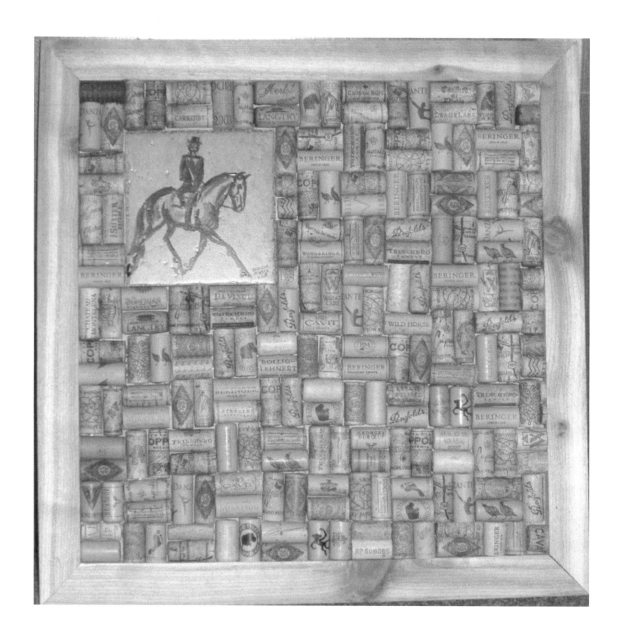

In this wall art you are able to see the diversity of the corks used, keeping the viewer's eyes on this work, simply reading corks and admiring.

This is an extremely large cork board using 650 corks and with a 6" x 6" hand painted tile insert. What FUN it was!

This piece hangs on the wall of our favorite pub in Sarasota, Florida at St. Armands Circle; "Lynches Pub and Grub" Our friends, Ethna and Chris, the owners, have provided wine corks from their Pub for most of my projects. Thank you girlfriends!

Visit this really fun Irish Pub for lunch, dinner or drinks when   you're on Florida's Southwestern Gulf Coast!

Ethna and Darlene

Project #4:   Textured Wall Art

Textured Wall Art simply refers to the imagination of embellishment. Now that you have completed a unique wall art piece from wine corks, you are ready to add more excitement to your work. Usually these projects are directed toward specific people or events. You have a direction for embellishing. I always like to say more is better. As you will see in this project my imagination ran wild. I purchased items, many more than I needed, and changed my arrangement several times. The excess embellishments will always be used in a future project, so there is no waste.

Needs:

Frame only, without glass.

Lauan board to fit the back of the frame

Wood glue

Tacks and a hammer

Hot glue gun or hot glue melting pot

Hot glue sticks

Needle nose pliers

Cutting board

Cutting tool

MOD PODGE®

Picture hanger kit

Plastic gloves

Embellishments

Ready………………Set………………….Go!

Prepare the Frame, as depicted on pages 44 and 45.

Design your Masterpiece!

1. Draw the design.

2. Lay out the embellishments from your design drawing. It may change after adding all you have. Decide which items express the best of your intended goal.

In this original design, I drew two wine bottles, however after placing these items inside the frame, there was only space for one. So plans change, as I said. Adapt and over-come.

The theme for this project is sentimental for my sister, Rita, to remember the good times with her daughter, Rhonda. I wanted to include my niece's friends and favorite gathering place. The corks and cork screw used in this project belonged to Rhonda.

The idea is a pub counter including the wine glass coasters, wine glasses, the mirror showing friends and mementoes of the fun times.

3.   Glue a base line of corks at the bottom. This is the counter space.

The corks for the wine bottle will be arranged several times before the gluing begins.

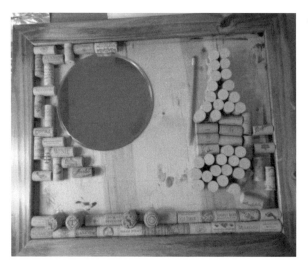

4.   Place your design of corks into the frame to again visualize your project.

Don't be surprised if you change the design or cork use, such as using champagne corks instead of wine corks for this bottle's label area, as I did.

5.   Start gluing the corks into place around the largest insert first. Here, the mirror is not attached yet due to spacing. Continue attaching whole corks to complete the patterns.

Whoops – *I made a mistake!*

Here it is….

My pattern was a Subway pattern for the lower base line section and a Heringbone pattern for the upper portion. This gives the effect of a counter top and back wall. However, I did not continue the Subway pattern to the right side of the bottle.

These corks were removed and re-glued into the correct pattern.

Below is the completed cork pattern for the backing of the embellishments to follow.

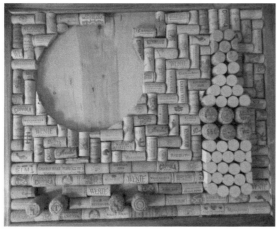

(Playing with the embellishments for the exciting part.)

6.   To emphasize the wine bottle in my design, I painted the ends of these corks a deep maroon. The champagne corks represent the label and gold glitter glued on the ends of the upper bottle neck corks for its seal.

7.   The embellishments have been added to enhance the meaning of
      this project. Here we have what meant the most to my niece;
      Lynch's Irish Pub, friends, cats, good wine, being a wonderful
      sister, music, the University of Florida and loving her art. A
      wonderful artist she was. You may ask? What are the dollars
      for? Dollars are a tradition at the pub to write a date on and pin
      to the ceiling. These have her family's birthdays on them. She
      always remembered important dates in the most loving and
      caring way.

It's truly amazing once you start, how much you can express and how
much fun it is. Your heart and soul goes into each project for someone
else. It is so appreciated.

Project #5:   The Message Board

First decide where this board is to hang. The location will determine the size and shape of the project. Remember the number of corks available also determines the size.

The message board is to be made the same as the wall hanging, but with the "grease board insert". It's just seven easy steps at this point.

Needs:

Frame only – no glass

Lauan plywood board to fit the back of the frame.

Grease board, chalk board or tablet.

Tacks and a hammer.

Corks – natural or synthetic

Wood glue

Hot glue gun and Hot glue melting pot

Glue sticks

Needle-nose pliers'

Cutting tool and cutting board

Wall screws

Picture hanger kit or wall screws

Plastic gloves

Embellishments

READY…………………..SET……………………..GO!

First: Prepare the Frame, as described on pages 44 and 45

1. Cut the Lauan plywood board to fit the back of the frame.
2. Glue the Lauan board in place.
3. Tack the board to the back of the frame.
4. Wipe off the excess glue from the edges.

Second: Lay out the design with the grease board in place.

Third: Arrange the corks in the desired pattern. Note that the champagne corks work well too, leaving space for the message board.

Forth: Attach the grease board to the lauan board backing with wood glue, hot glue or screws, depending on the size, weight and composition. This is done first, due to the large sizes of most grease boards.

Fifth: Now begin gluing the corks in place. It's best to use the needle -nose pliers' to hold the corks and dip them into the hot glue pot on their sides.

Sixth: As with the wall hanging, now cut the corks to fit the small spaces and glue them in place.

Seventh: Finally decide the wall attachment method. The message board must not move when being written on by the user, thus it is best to simply attach the board into the wall surface at all four corners.

Note: This completed message board was for a beach condo kitchen wall with a nautical theme. Tile ends were glued onto the board to match the kitchen tile. The entire completed project was actually screwed into the wall at the inside of each corner, (can you find the screws?), thus it can be removed, placed somewhere else and the kitchen wall redesigned.

Embellishments again add useful items, such as the seahorse key hook and the champagne corks for a tacking notes section.

NOW WRITE...... *"I'M DONE AND HAVE CREATED A USEFUL ITEM!"*

Project #6:

The Round Frame for Photos, Mirrors or Clocks

Enough of the square stuff. Let's think outside the box. It's your turn now to explode your creative talents. GO FOR IT!

This is the project to put that WOW factor into your work. Make a gift for that someone special in your life. I'm making this for my special girlfriend who always puts a smile on my face. We will call her "Wild Thing!"

The round design first starts with your project desire, photo frame, mirror frame or clock. All will start with going to your local hobby or lumber supply store to purchase the round wooden disc, or you may have a means to cut a circle from board, again lauan plywood board works great!

Remember, the size of your round frame base will depend on the number of corks you have, the size of your photo, mirror or clock and where it is to hang. Is this piece to match another art layout or to accent a wall design?

Shop for embellishments! That's the real fun.

<u>Note:</u> In this project there may be spaces between the corks in a circle, so decide if you would like to stain or paint the base frame board. These spaces may be visible in your design. The larger the circle, the less space will be noticed. Of course also, the larger the circle, the more corks you'll need.

Needs:

Backing circle frame

Photo, mirror or clock

Corks, a mixture of natural and synthetic will do and colors are nice attention pieces

MOD PODGE® for a photo

Mirror mastic for a mirror

Velcro or Magnets for a clock, as it has to be removed to change batteries and set the time.

Hot glue melting pot

Glue sticks

Needle-nose pliers

Cutting tool and Cutting board

Picture hanger kit

Plastic gloves

Embellishments!

READY……………………..SET…………………….GO!

Lay it all out and design again. This is all about you and your imagination.

In FIVE easy steps!

<u>First:</u> Prepare the frame base …This can also be done after the cork pattern layout.

    1. **Did you decide to stain or paint it?**

    2. **Do NOT attach the picture hanger kit yet.**

<u>Second</u>:   Lay out your design…

1.   **You may want the corks side by side like this layout of the Circle Sunray Pattern.**

In using this pattern, try to arrange the smaller ends of the corks to the center of the circle for a tighter pattern and less spaces. The larger ends of the corks should be to the outside of the circle pattern. This is a 12" diameter circle and requires 34 corks.

2.   **Or the corks could go end to end in the Circle Stack Pattern. In this arrangement another row of corks can be glued on top and between the first two rows for an enhanced 3-D appearance.**

Two rows require 33 corks and with the third optional row on top between the two bottom rows, it requires 50 corks.

3. Before continuing, insert your chosen item to check for the fit.

Then trace around the clock onto the circle frame in order to maintain a gluing guide for the corks. Once the corks are glued they cannot be moved to fit your item within the circle.

Third: Glue the corks onto the base circle

1. Begin hot gluing the corks in place. I suggest doing this before inserting your item as the hot glue tends to drip glue strings onto the intended insert.

2. You may also wish to cut small sections of corks to fill in larger spaces. This is to be done now.

Forth: Attach the Picture hanger kit to the back.

Finally: Insert your item
    With the appropriate adhesive, attach your item inside the circle and embellish! The clock insert simply sets inside the corks with a tight fit, thus easily removed for battery replacement. My girlfriend will also be able to attach her personal embellishments to the corks with stick pins!

AMAZING, there is nothing else like this personal, useful art clock and it just keeps getting embellished as time goes on!

The wine glass can be detached and used to celebrate!

CONGRATULATIONS!

WOW !

I told you that as soon as someone saw your beautiful art with corks, you will receive special requests!

Guess what? Before this manual was completed, it happened and look at the "Happy Face!"

Alison wanted her own special themed clock in her colors, thus, it displays all she is….a horse lover, cowgirl, daughter of a minister and a country girl who loves "Duck Dynasty" wine.

"Make someone happy today!"

Project #7: Cork Castle Aquarium

      This perhaps is the most ambitious and creative project. Time, skill and patience are your greatest assets for creating your own unique "Cork Castle Aquarium." Upon completion add your favorite colored male Betta and enjoy watching him peer through the windows and flaring his beautiful fins. A Betta is recommended due to this species of fish being air breathers, thus the usual aquarium pump system is not required. A glass container with ample air space works well. It's your time to relax and enjoy all you have created while your new pet enjoys a new home.

Needs:

      Corks, a combination will do fine, wine and champagne, natural and synthetic.

      A large diameter glass cylinder container

      A smaller diameter glass cylinder container

      (Both need to be the same height with at least a 3 inch difference in their diameters so the smaller will slide inside the larger with clearance for the cork castle to slide over it.)

      Aquarium stones or glass colored beads

      Poster paper, your color choice

      Package tape

      Hot glue pot

      Hot glue gun

      Hot glue sticks

      Needle-nose plyers'

Plastic gloves

Cutting tool and cutting board

Colored marker, same color as the poster paper

Aluminum foil

Caulk

Scissors, small cut

Razor knife for paper

Bottled pure water

Betta fish

Betta food

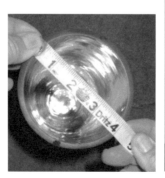

Are You Ready?....Let's Get Started!

1. Lay the poster paper flat and place the smaller cylinder across the end. Roll the poster paper around the cylinder.

2. Over lap the poster paper ends, draw a line on the paper along the rolled cylinder, then cut the poster paper.

3. Roll the poster paper again over the smaller cylinder and tape loosely closed. Stand up the cylinder.

4. Add the aquarium rocks inside the cylinder for stability while gluing the corks. Slide the rolled poster paper over the glass tube.

5.	Stand the wrapped cylinder on top of the aluminum foil. Aluminum foil is used because it is easier to pull from the corks should the hot glue attach the gluing surface to the cork base.

6.	Use corks of the same length to encircle the base of the covered cylinder. Glue to the poster paper.

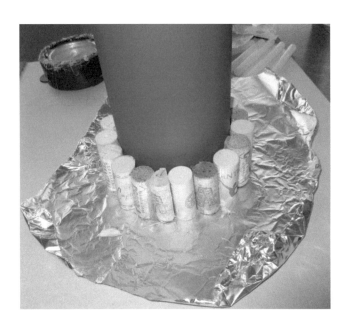

The hot glue gun may be better for the rounded surfaces, allowing more contact.

7.   Now you have a clean surface to begin your pattern. Let me
     suggest a spiral pattern to enhance the cylinder shape. In my
     piece, the pattern simulates the staircase of the castle's tower
     using champagne corks. I continued this around the top for the
     castle's crown. The champagne corks must be cut off at the neck
     so only the tops are used. Now use the caulk to draw your own
     pattern onto the poster board. You may try several and
     simply erase the ones you don't want. Glue the corks on the
     pattern selected. Since non glued areas will be cut away, make
     sure the upper corks have support.

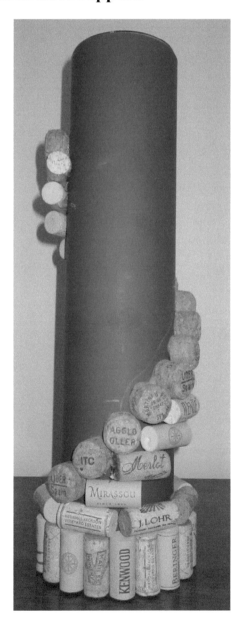

8.   Glue the corks. Most can be dipped in the hot glue pot, however
      as shown previous, some will need the use of the hot glue gun to
      add glue to the cork sides for support. Remember, you are gluing
      on a rounded surface.

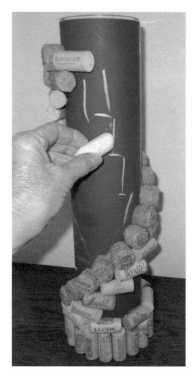 

9.   Cutting your castle windows is the next step. Take the razor knife and follow the edge of the corks. Gently cut to the glass surface without scaring the glass.

10.   Peel the poster paper pieces from the pattern.

11.   You will be amazed how your castle tower is forming. Remove the cork castle wrap from the cylinder by lifting it straight up. Take the small scissors and slowly trim each cut area to clean the edges. As few as possible paper edges should show from the outside.

12.   Take the colored marker which is the same color as the poster paper and color the edges so no white paper can be seen.

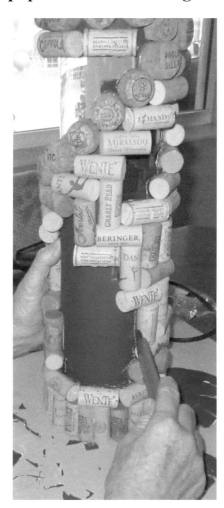

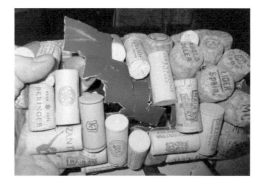

13. **Place the smaller diameter cylinder inside the larger diameter cylinder.**

14. **Slide the newly created cork castle down over the smaller diameter cylinder which is now inside the larger one. The larger cylinder is used for a more dimensional appearance and support of the glued castle. Look at your work one last time and make sure you are happy before it becomes your Betta home. If you are happy, remove the cork castle by lifting it up and out before filling with water. Doing this will keep it dry.**

15. Fill the smaller cylinder with pure water and let it set for two hours.

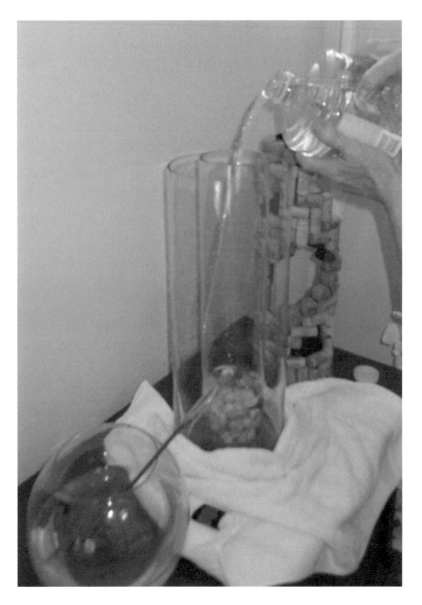

16. Welcome your Betta to his new home. Feed him. A pinch of Betta food   will do.

Now that was a project…….

Congratulations and Enjoy!

Cleaning the Cork Castle Aquarium

Your Betta will enjoy a clean home once a week. Remember, there is no filter system, thus cleaning is important, but not complicated.

1.   Remove your cork castle by lifting it straight up and set it aside.

2.   Catch and remove your Betta, placing him in a prepared bowl. He will only be there for a couple of hours while the new water settles.

3.   Lift the smaller cylinder straight up and empty, clean and sit back inside the larger cylinder.

4.   Add pure water and let set for two hours.

5.   Slide the cork castle over the filled cylinder.

6.   Let your Betta return home a happy fish. Feed.

 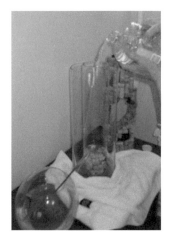

Explode Your Imagination!

If you see and think it, you can do it!

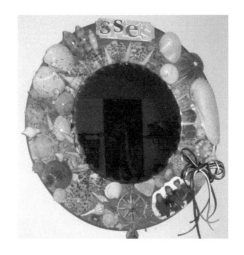

Remember, You See it, You can do it and More!

I know you can!

Thank you for sharing time and your talents with me. I'm looking forward to more fun with future art projects, as above: shell art, painting on gourds, acrylics and oils. *V. Darlene Geiser*

Index

MOD PODGE, 37, 39, 44, 46, 58, 70,

Printed in the United States
By Bookmasters